Copyright © by Harcourt, Inc.

All rights reserved. No part of this publication may be reproduced or transmitted in any form or by any means, electronic or mechanical, including photocopy, recording, or any information storage and retrieval system, without permission in writing from the publisher.

Permission is hereby granted to individual teachers using the corresponding student's textbook or kit as the major vehicle for regular classroom instruction to photocopy complete pages from this publication in classroom quantities for instructional use and not for resale. Requests for information on other matters regarding duplication of this work should be addressed to School Permissions and Copyrights, Harcourt, Inc., 6277 Sea Harbor Drive, Orlando, Florida 32887-6777. Fax: 407-345-2418.

HARCOURT and the Harcourt Logo are trademarks of Harcourt, Inc., registered in the United States of America and/or other jurisdictions.

Grateful acknowledgment is made to Clarion Books, a Houghton Mifflin Company imprint for permission to reprint the cover illustration from *Feast for 10* by Cathryn Falwell. Copyright © 1993 by Cathryn Falwell.

Printed in the United States of America

ISBN 0-15-325083-6

1 2 3 4 5 6 7 8 9 10   1421   10 09

Illustration Credits
Ken Bowser, 5–6, 10, 15–16, 18, 23–24; Bart Rivers, 7, 20–21; Linda Davick, 8–9, 18; Mercedes McDonald, 11; Len Epstein, 12; Chris Reed, 13–14, 17, 19, 22.

Homework

☐ Plan a healthy meal with your family. Include foods from each of the food groups.	☐ Help a family member make up a grocery list.	☐ Draw pictures of things that begin with the letter *p*.
☐ Talk about your favorite foods with a family member.	☐ Draw pictures of things whose names end with the letter *p*.	☐ Play "I Spy" with your family. Look for things whose names begin with *p*.
☐ Draw pictures of things whose names begin with the letter *c*.	☐ Play "I Spy" with your family. Look for things whose names begin with *c*.	☐ Draw a picture to show something you like to do. Ask a family member to help you write an action word to describe your picture.
☐ Play "Simon Says" with your family.	☐ With a family member, name as many foods as you can think of whose names have the letter *p* or *c*.	☐ Think of rhyming words for *am*.
☐ Get a take-out menu from a restaurant. Circle each letter *a*, *p*, and *c* on the menu.	☐ Think of rhyming words for *at*.	☐ Re-read the Fold-Up Book to a family member.

Around the Table

My Letters

My Words

I like

Books to Share

Feast for Ten by Cathryn Falwell.
Clarion Books, 1993.

Little Red Hen by Byron Barton.
HarperCollins, 1993.

Lunch by Denise Fleming.
Henry Holt, 1999.

Around the Table

Eat the sandwich!

SCHOOL-HOME CONNECTION
Read the story to your child and talk about how the sandwich was made.

8

Squash the. . .

cup

bread

grapes

spoon

6

3

Response to Literature: *Peanut Butter and Jelly*
Help children assemble the book. Read the pages and have children circle the appropriate items to retell the story.

Around the Table 5

Bake the...

2

hat   apples

glass   grapes

7

Mash the...

4

plate   bread

peanuts   knife

5

6 Around the Table

Name _____

P P p p

☐at's ☐icnic

Consonant: *Pp*
Have children trace and write *P* and *p*. Have them find and mark *P* and *p* on the page. Children can complete the words with *Pp*.

Around the Table 7

Name _____

Relating /p/ to p
Have children circle the picture in each row whose name begins with the /p/ sound. Then have them print P or p beside the correct picture.

8 Around the Table

Name _____

  .

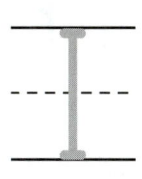   .

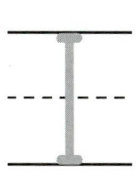   .

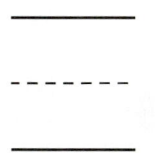   .

High-Frequency Word: *I*
Have children trace the word *I* in the first three sentences and then read them. Have children write *I* in the last sentence and complete it by drawing a food they love to eat. Ask children to read their sentences.

Around the Table   9

Name _____

C C c c

☐ooking ☐orner

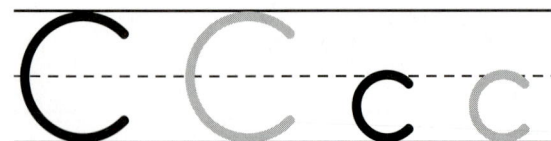

Cake Pans   Cookie Cutters   Cups

cake   cookies

Consonant: Cc
Discuss the page and read the words. Have children trace over the letters C and c. Then have them find and mark each C and c on the page. Children can complete the words with C or c.

10 Around the Table

Name _____

I like 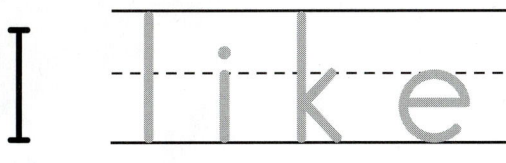 .

I like  .

I like  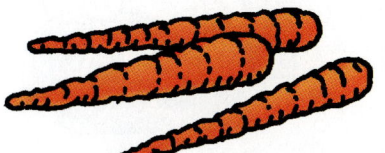 .

I _____  .

High-Frequency Word: *like*
Have children trace the word *like* in the first three sentences. Have children write *like* in the last sentence and complete it by drawing a favorite food. Ask children to read their sentences.

Around the Table 11

Name _____

Relating /k/ to c
Ask children to name each item on the computer monitor. Have them write C or c beside the items that begin with the /k/ sound.

Around the Table

Name _____

Consonants: *Cc, Pp*
Have children name each picture and listen for the beginning sound. Ask them to write *c* if the picture name begins with the /k/ sound, or *p* if the picture name begins with the /p/ sound.

Around the Table 13

Name _____

I  eat ____.

  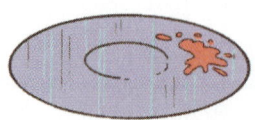

I  sip ____.

 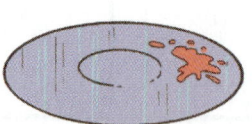 

I  wash ____.

Focus Skill: Action Words
Read the sentence starters with children and identify the pictures. Have children circle the picture that best completes each sentence. Then have children read the sentences.

Around the Table

Name _____

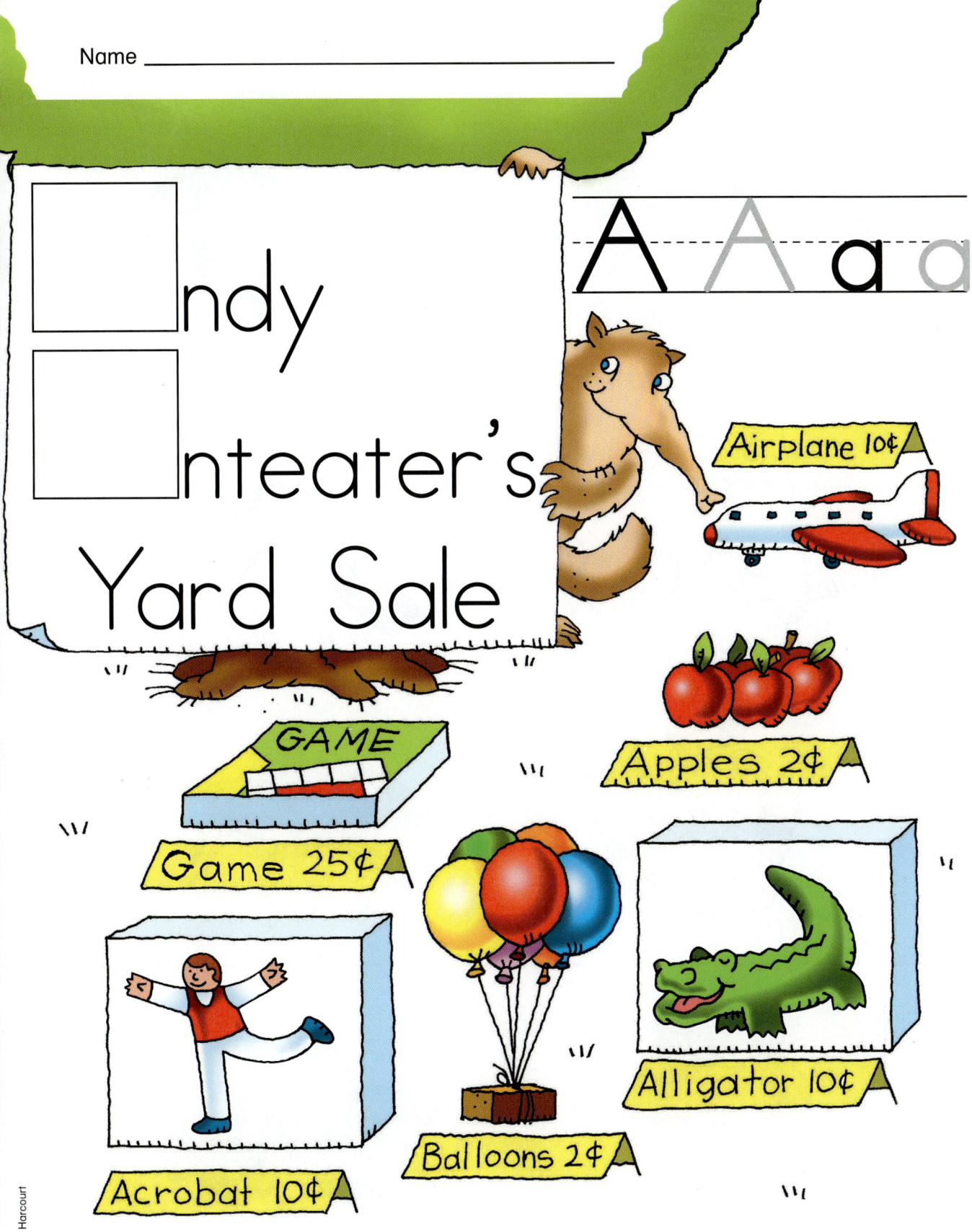

Vowel: *Aa*
Discuss the pictures with children and read the words. Have children trace over the letters *A* and *a* and find and mark each one on the page. Children can complete the words with *A* or *a*.

Around the Table 15

Name _____

Relating /a/ to a
Have children circle the picture in each row whose name begins with the /a/ sound. Then have them write A or a beside the correct picture.

16 Around the Table

Name _____

Sam →

ram →

map →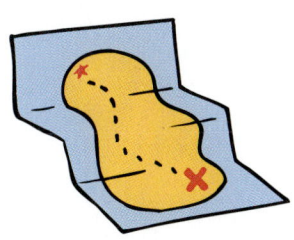

Blending *a – m*
Identify the pictures for children. Then have them read each word and circle the picture in each row that names the word.

Around the Table 17

Name _____

S a m likes  .

P_____ likes _____ .

The r_____ likes _____ .

Words with /a/ and /m/
Have children look at the picture, trace *am* in the first sentence and read it.
Have them complete the sentences with *am* and by drawing something each
character would like. Then have children read their sentences.

18 Around the Table

Name _____

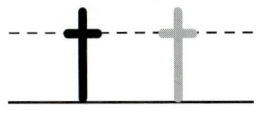  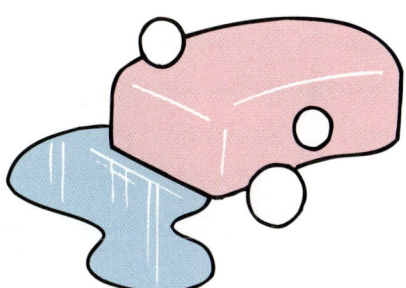

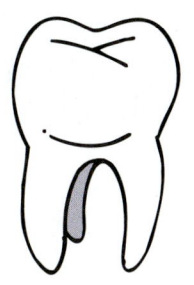 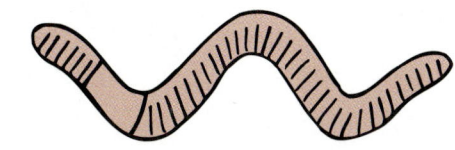

Consonant: /t/t, Short Vowel: /a/a
Have children name the letter in the first box and circle pictures whose names begin with the /a/ sound. Have children name the letter in the second box and circle pictures whose names begin with the /t/ sound.

Around the Table 19

Name _____

mat →

cat →

tap →

Blending a – t
Identify the pictures for children. Then have them read each word and circle the picture in each row that names the word.

20 Around the Table

Name _____

mat

tap

cat

Sam

Words with /a/ and /t/
Have children read the word, and then circle the picture that the word names.

Around the Table

Name _____

Pat sat.

The cat sat.

I tap.

I sat.

Blending a – t
Have children read the sentences and discuss the pictures. Then have them draw a picture to go with the last sentence, showing themselves sitting and doing a favorite activity.

The Toy Store

Name _____

I am Sam.

I like the cat.

Fold-Up Book
Help children cut out and fold the book. Then ask children to read the story with a partner.

SCHOOL-HOME CONNECTION
Have your child read the story. Talk about the kind of toy they would like to have from the shop.

2 I like the map.

3 I am Pat.

24 Around the Table